FIRE
Anna Skowrońska

Graphic design and illustrations by
Agata Dudek and Małgorzata Nowak

Translation by Antonia Lloyd-Jones

Boxer Books

While you're having dinner have you ever wondered who invented cooking and when? How come after sunset we don't have to sit in the dark? You'll find the answers in the remote history of our ancestors who learned how to domesticate fire. It gave them warmth, light and a sense of security. Today, very few people rely on fire to cook their food or light their homes. Over the centuries, fire has been industrialised. Now we send out a "spark" with the help of a high-tension wire and heat is provided to our homes by a thermal power station or a gasworks. But we still enjoy gazing into the flames of a fire or a candle. So what exactly is fire, the element that warms, lights and feeds us, but can also be extremely destructive?

WHAT IS FIRE?

Everything we can touch is made up of atoms that are constantly attracting or repelling one another. There are lots of them in the branches you gather for a bonfire, too. And although wood lies there quietly, its atoms are gently vibrating. However, you can't see that because they're too small, but you can imagine it. The composition of the branches includes atoms of carbon, while the air includes atoms of oxygen. While your branches are peacefully lying on the ground surrounded by air, the oxygen bounces off the carbon and nothing happens. But if you heat the wood, in other words provide it with energy, the atoms will start to vibrate intensely, moving faster and faster, bouncing off one another, and pushing one another until they start to combine violently with the oxygen. And in the process they will emit light. They will stir additional atoms in the wood to do more vibrating and the process keeps repeating until the fuel runs out. It is then, when carbon atoms from your sticks combine violently with oxygen atoms from the air, that fire is produced. But there has to be a great many of them all at once.

The American physicist Richard Feynman said that a log on a bonfire is a "sort of stored sun that comes out when you burn it". He explained that every dry twig was once part of a tree. A spruce, a birch or a pine have spent years sourcing carbon dioxide from the air, but to divide the carbon from the oxygen inside them, they have borrowed energy from the sun. When their timber is set alight, and the carbon combines with oxygen again, they give back the energy that they borrowed in the past.

RICHARD FEYNMAN

Heat

When you cook food on a campfire or stand around a fire pit, what do you feel? The particles of gases from burning wood move very fast and prompt the particles of your body to vibrate, and then you feel heat. The faster the particles of gases, liquids or solids are vibrating and moving, the higher their temperature.

For fire to be produced we must have something that provides the initial energy (a spark or a flame), fuel (wood, paper or petrol), and oxygen, which combines with gases in combustion. Some substances can ignite of their own accord, which we call spontaneous combustion.

STICKS

DRY LEAVES

LOGS

PAPER

MATCHES

The shape of a flame

In the process of combustion, oxidising gases are heated. Their particles move faster and push in all directions, occupying more space. That's why hot air has less density, is lighter and starts to rise. This happens when the force of gravity is at work. This is what affects the shape of a flame. NASA (National Aeronautics and Space Administration), the American space agency, conducted an experiment on a space station where the force of gravity is very small. The astronauts lit a flame, which had a different shape than on earth – it was shaped like a ball, not a teardrop.

The colour of a flame

The Kawah Ijen Volcano in Indonesia shines blue at night. Tongues of fire flicker on its slopes and in its crevices. You may ask why they are not orange, as usual. The intense blue colour of the flames comes from burning sulphur fumes that emerge from inside the volcano.

The colour of a flame depends on the chemical composition of the fuel. Sulphur is yellow, but it burns with a blue flame; wood is brown but it burns orange; copper is reddish in colour, but its flame is blue-green. If you'd like your birthday cake to burn with multi-coloured flames, you have to buy special candles, each of which has a different chemical composition. They can all be the same colour – what matters is what they were made of.

Fireworks

You've probably seen firework displays where the fireworks produced flashes of multi-coloured light against a dark-blue sky. Their colours depend on chemical compounds. Calcium tints the flame red, lithium turns it fuchsia pink, sodium makes it orange, sulphur turns it blue and potassium makes it lilac.

Take a close look at the flame of a gas cooker and you'll notice that it's usually blue. But sometimes it burns yellow and red, which means the cooker isn't working properly – the combustion is incomplete.

LIKE A BOLT OUT OF THE BLUE

As you read this book, more than 2,000 thunderstorms are happening around the world! Perhaps there's one approaching your home? If we could harness the energy of one single storm, we could charge a billion AA batteries or light a city larger than Birmingham for half an hour. A storm occurs when ice crystals in the clouds collide with one another and with tiny drops of water, and pick up static electricity. The positively charged drops gather at the top of the cloud, while the negatively charged ones remain at the bottom. Once both these areas are sufficiently charged, a violent electric current flows through the cloud and a thunderbolt strikes. We see it in the form of lightning.

Flashes of lightning can have different colours: red, blueish or yellow. Their colour depends on air pollution, humidity and air temperature.

Try brushing your hair vigorously with a plastic comb or brush. You'll see that your hair starts to stand on end. That means the rubbing has caused it to pick up static electricity, like the drops of water and ice crystals in a cloud.

Most lightning discharges happen between clouds, but they can also run between a cloud and the Earth. On the Earth, positive charges concentrate around objects that stick up, such as tall towers, trees, or people if they are standing in an open space. That is where lightning is most likely to strike so you must never stand under a tree or a tall post during a storm. If possible, take shelter in a building or a car. And switch off your mobile phone. Even if you're sitting safely at home, don't use electrical appliances.

A bolt of lightning is very hot, at around 30,000°C. When it strikes, the air temperature rises abruptly and the air expands and vibrates. That's when we hear thunder. If the lightning hits a tree, the heat from it can turn its sap into steam and make its trunk explode. Lightning can set off fires.

During a single lightning strike so much energy is released that it could power your computer non-stop for more than a year.

Perhaps the most famous lightning bolt in literature is the one on Harry Potter's forehead, the mark left on him by a terrible spell. But the most famous mythological character to hurl thunderbolts is Zeus, the ancient Greek god.

VOLCANOES
Red sky

Perhaps you have read the story of the Little Prince, who carefully cleaned volcanoes so they'd burn without erupting? As he cooked his breakfast on them, he wanted the flame to burn steadily. But it would be hard to cook your food on a real volcano! However in March 2021, after a volcano that had been inactive for more than 800 years erupted in Iceland, local people cooked sausages in cracks in the solidified lava.

The "roots" of volcanoes reach deep inside the Earth, where rocks melt at a high temperature. A hot, fluid mass is formed, which mixes with gases and water vapour, and under pressure seeks an outlet. We call the point where it finds an exit to the Earth's surface a volcano. Molten lava, which can be as hot as 1,250°C, pours down the slopes of the mountain, and gases, dust and volcanic ash are thrown into the air at immense speed. As a result, we can imagine just how hot it is inside the Earth. Today, there are systems that can predict an eruption and warn people. Nevertheless, it is still possible to be taken by surprise. Because of the extreme force they displayed, in ancient times volcanoes were thought to have divine qualities. The name "volcano" comes from Vulcan, the Roman god of fire and metalworking. The Greeks called him Hephaestus and believed that his smithy was inside a volcano, where among other things he forged thunderbolts for Zeus.

Some of the volcanoes in Iceland lie within an ice zone. The eruptions in this region are doubly dangerous because the high temperature causes glaciers to melt abruptly, resulting in floods.

Some of the islands between Asia and Australia are home to birds that do not sit on their eggs but give the task to . . . a volcano. The New Guinea scrubfowl, which looks a bit like a chicken, builds its nest close to a volcanic crater, where it's extremely hot. They look for places where the temperature will be no more or less than 33°C. They are so good at sensing the temperature, it's as if they have built-in thermometers. They use their powerful feet to dig in the sand and earth and, once they're sure they've found a warm enough spot, they bury their eggs and take no further interest in them. Sixty days later, fully fledged chicks hatch and immediately fly off into the world.

Along the shores of the Pacific Ocean for more than 40,000 kilometres there is a chain of volcanoes, volcanic islands and oceanic trenches. It is known as the Ring of Fire.

CROSS SECTION OF A VOLCANO

When a volcano erupts, not just toxic gases enter the atmosphere but also vast quantities of dust that the wind then carries over great distances. Sometimes the concentration of dust is so high that it can damage aeroplane engines. For this reason, in 2010 a volcanic eruption put air traffic on hold in Europe for several days.

In 1883, the Indonesian volcano Krakatoa threw such a vast amount of dust into the atmosphere that for several years the appearance of the sky changed worldwide. Sunsets were so red that they looked like the afterglow of a fire – in New York someone even summoned the fire brigade! The moon, on the other hand, took on a shade of blue or green.

Darkness

Over the Bay of Naples the sky is azure blue and the sun shines brightly for most of the year. More than 2,000 years ago the city of Pompeii was built there. Rich Romans walked around the perfectly designed forum, looking in one direction at Mount Vesuvius, which dominated the city, and in the other at the Mediterranean Sea. The city was large and wealthy, with about 10,000 inhabitants. They commissioned the best artists to decorate their houses with colourful paintings, and their floors with mosaics in complicated patterns. They cultivated vineyards and olive groves. They enjoyed the theatre, banquets and gladiator fights.

In the year 79 CE, darkness suddenly covered the area. The famous Pompeian azure sky went grey. The historian Pliny the Younger, who at the time was living on the other side of the bay, described how the darkness was as intense as in a closed room where the lamp has suddenly gone out. However, the darkness was not caused by ordinary clouds, but ash and smoke rising from Vesuvius. The burning hot stones that it spat out fell on the city and set the buildings on fire. Toxic gases escaped from underground and soon it was impossible to breathe. In a short time, the people, animals and houses were all petrified forever, buried beneath a layer of dust several metres deep. It was only 1,700 years later that Pompeii was discovered, and the excavation is still going on today.

DISCOVERY

Today as you watch flashes of lightning illuminate the night, remember that two million years ago when they cut across the sky, our ancestors looked at them in terror. They were seeing fire, but they didn't know what caused it. There was a prehistoric human being who lived in Africa 2.5 million years ago. He was named Homo habilis, meaning 'handy human.' He had thick hair that covered his body. He didn't know how to light a bonfire to keep himself warm. He ate raw vegetables, fruit and meat. He didn't cook or fry them – he didn't know how. We don't know whether he hunted, because the tools found beside him were very simple and could only have been used to cut up animals that had already been killed by predators. The only fire he knew was the kind that set things alight by falling from the sky or emerging from underground. It's possible that he did make use of it, if he was able to keep the embers glowing that were left by burned grass and bushes. He knew that it meant he didn't have to sit in the dark after nightfall. He used fire occasionally, if nature helped him to do so, but he had no idea how to kindle it for himself.

AUSTRALOPITHECUS
APPROX 3.8–2.9 MILLION YEARS AGO

HOMO HABILIS
APPROX 2.4–1.5 MILLION YEARS AGO

HOMO ERECTUS
APPROX 1.7 MILLION–200,000 YEARS AGO

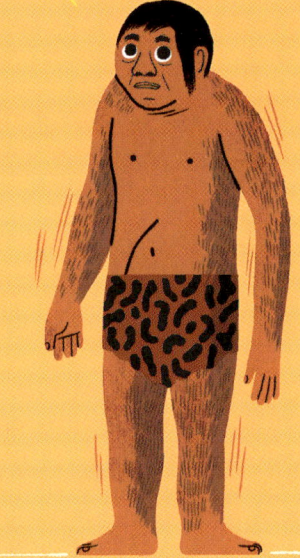

HOMO FLORESIENSIS
APPROX 100,000–50,000 YEARS AGO

Heat

How did human beings come up with the idea of controlling fire? Who first managed to do it? No one knows. The origins of domesticating fire are lost in the mists of time. What we do know is that this discovery speeded up the development of humankind. Now not just the day was bright, but it became easier to see at night by the light of a bonfire. People gathered around the flames that gave them heat and light, and scared away predators. They felt safer. They learned to cook and to make tools and weapons, and simply spent time together around the dancing flames. They talked, told stories and took care of their children. The bonds between them became stronger and a community was formed.

HOMO HEIDELBERGENSIS
APPROX 600,000–250,000 YEARS AGO

NEANDERTHAL MAN
APPROX 130,000–40,000 YEARS AGO

HOMO SAPIENS
APPROX 300,000 YEARS AGO TO THE PRESENT

The ancient Greeks believe that humans got fire from Prometheus, who stole it from sacred Mount Olympus. For this deed, Zeus, king of the gods, condemned him to eternal torment. He had Prometheus chained to a rock in the Caucasus Mountains, where every day an eagle flew down to tear out his liver.

Roasted antelope

In time, people realised that they could prepare food on a fire. The roasted meat and vegetables that were added to the menu had a basic virtue – they were more digestible than raw ones. Now the human body needed less time to digest and could assign the energy saved to the development of the brain. Gradually the stomach became smaller, the intestines shorter, and the well-nourished brain grew larger, capable of serving "thinking man", in other words Homo sapien.

The flames of bonfires lit up the caverns and passages of extensive caves, which had been inaccessible before then because there was no light in them. Now they served as comfortable living quarters where people could shelter from the rain and cold. They also began to seek new places to live, because now that they could get warm easily, they were no longer as dependent on a warm climate. Gradually they migrated from Africa to Asia and Europe.

Smoked meat

Hunters learned to use fire for hunting. They also made better wooden tools, hardened by fire, which allowed them to catch and kill game. Formerly, they had rarely eaten meat and generally tore it from animals that a predator had already hunted. Now they had so much of it that some was wasted. They sought ways to preserve food and found out they could smoke it over a bonfire, or in special hearths. Now it was easier for them to move from place to place, because the smoked meat was like the canned food we use for camping.

People learned to set bushes on fire to prepare the ground for cultivation. The resulting ash made ideal fertiliser, and edible plants grew quickly on the scorched meadows. Burning also helped to combat insects.

Once human beings had learned to kindle fire, they began to devise better ways of using it, and to develop technology. First they invented clay vessels that they baked on a bonfire, and then ovens in which the vessels were made. In time they perfected these ovens, using them to smelt metal and make tools, weapons and bronze vessels. Next they made ovens for smelting a very durable material – iron. We can trace the history of the development of technology thousands of years back in time to its source, which is the domestication of fire.

If it weren't for fire, we wouldn't have any window panes. Glass is made in smelting ovens shaped like huge bathtubs. A combination of quartz sand and other raw materials is placed into the oven and heated to a temperature of around 1,500°C until it melts. Then glasses, bottles and panes are formed out of it. The kind of glass produced depends on the composition of its raw materials. It's a very ecological material. Once made, it can be melted and shaped a second time.

Pasta is cooked in light steel pots, but how did our ancestors cook their food? The oldest pots we know about today were found in China, where they were made around 20,000 years ago. They were made of clay, but weren't very skilfully fired, so they broke easily. In those days, people were not only unaware of pasta but hadn't yet learned to cultivate plants or produce flour. Ever since Xianren Cave was discovered in 1960, archaeologists have been digging up more and more fragments of the broken vessels.

EXPLORERS OF THE PAST

Lunch at Terra Amata

In August on the south coast of France near Nice, it's hard to find space on the beach. Crowds besiege the restaurants, bars and cafés. There you can order duck à l'orange, seafood, and pizza, of course, and for dessert chocolate mousse. But 400,000 years ago you'd have eaten roasted venison or rhinoceros. Hunters lived in this area and their cuisine was definitely less refined. They knew how to hunt and then roast the meat they caught. We know this thanks to the work of a team headed by Professor Henry de Lumley, who discovered one of the world's oldest hearths at a place called Terra Amata on the outskirts of Nice. As a result, we can be sure that 400,000 years ago people already knew how to use fire. Similar discoveries have been made in Brittany, England, Hungary and China.

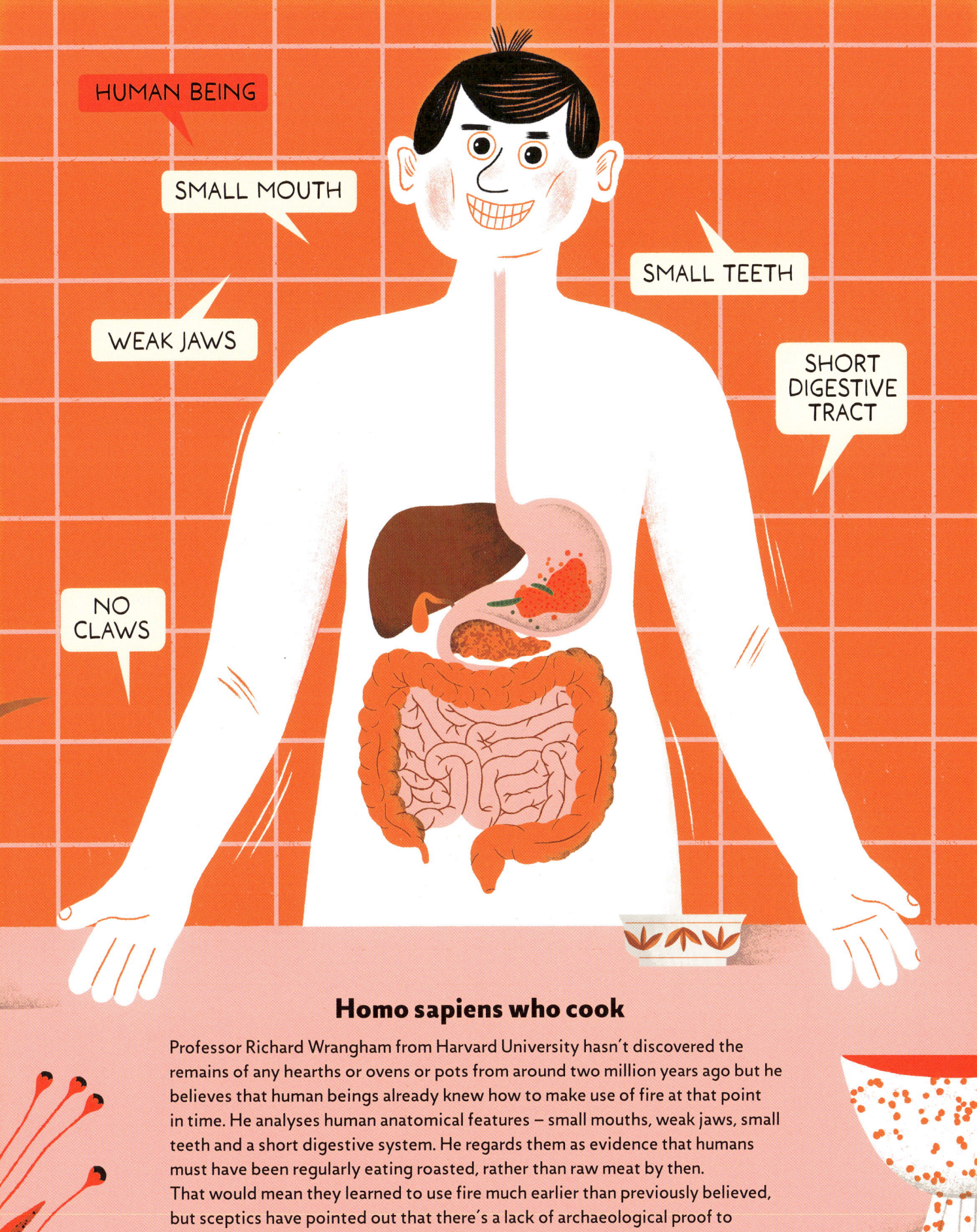

Homo sapiens who cook

Professor Richard Wrangham from Harvard University hasn't discovered the remains of any hearths or ovens or pots from around two million years ago but he believes that human beings already knew how to make use of fire at that point in time. He analyses human anatomical features – small mouths, weak jaws, small teeth and a short digestive system. He regards them as evidence that humans must have been regularly eating roasted, rather than raw meat by then.
That would mean they learned to use fire much earlier than previously believed, but sceptics have pointed out that there's a lack of archaeological proof to confirm this theory.

Research

If you wanted to know what dishes your parents or grandparents ate during their childhood, you'd only have to ask them. You can find out how cooking was done before then by reading memoirs, letters and diaries. But how can you learn about life on Earth in the days when there was no writing or language? That's the job of archaeologists, anthropologists and others who research the past. For them, the equivalent of diaries are animal fossils, pieces of bone, the remains of plants that died out hundreds of thousands of years ago, sand, stones and geological deposits. First, they look for this sort of evidence and then they laboriously piece it all together, like a jigsaw puzzle to form a single whole. But that is not always the end of the work, because sometimes one of the pieces of the puzzle turns out to have been put in the wrong place.

In 1925, some pieces of bone were discovered in South Africa that were more than three million years old. They seemed to be charred, so it looked as if some extremely ancient evidence of fire had been found. But when they were sent to a chemical laboratory, their black colour turned out to be from iron oxide, and they bore no traces of fire at all. These bones belonged to Australopithecus and were found in the Makapan Valley.

Scientists are continually developing more advanced methods for studying fossils, bones, and the remains of plants from millions of years ago. Electron microscopes can examine the tiniest details. Computer tomographs and X-rays reveal the internal structure of the remains under analysis. Specialised computer programmes can create visualisations. In 1981, tools and animal remains from Olduvai Gorge in Tanzania came under the microscope. The scientists noticed cut marks on some of the bones that must have been made by a stone tool, but they also noticed the tooth marks of predators. So they realised that Homo habilis had not hunted game, but simply cut up the meat of animals that were already dead when they were found.

Chemical research conducted in a laboratory can determine the temperature reached by burned remains, and can also help to discover what the earliest human beings ate.

Sparks

Today we can light up a room with a single flick of a switch. Prehistoric people had to spend ages rubbing sticks together. Eventually the sticks grew hot enough to ignite. Sometimes this task had to be repeated over and over again because it wasn't instantly possible to set dry grass or twigs alight. People had to be very patient. And when they finally did manage to light a fire, they were very careful not to let it go out. We cannot define exactly when and where human beings learned to kindle fire, but they must have kept searching for new and easier methods.

Flint, touchwood and steel, the firelighters of the past

Flint is a kind of stone. Touchwood is powdered bracket fungus – which grows on trees – or anything that's easily set alight (such as down, catkins, or dry leaves). A steel fire starter is a tool made of steel. For centuries these items formed the basic set of tools for kindling fire. It wasn't at all easy. The steel was systematically struck against flint, producing sparks, which, if everything succeeded, landed on the touchwood and set it alight.

FLINT
STEEL
← TOUCHWOOD
TWO PIECES OF WOOD

Pyrite

Pyrite is a dark-yellow stone. Its name comes from the Greek word *pyr*, meaning fire. It was used to kindle fire in the days when people had not yet discovered iron. They struck or rubbed flint against pyrite, producing a spark. Sometimes this left deep grooves in the flint, which show how many times the activity was repeated. In 1991, German tourists stumbled upon a frozen body in mountains in the Tyrol region. It didn't occur to them that they had found the remains of a man who lived 5,300 years ago. Among the many objects found with him were flints and the remains of a bracket fungus with traces of pyrite, which he must have used to kindle fire. He was given the name Ötzi the Ice Man.

PYRITE

Evidence of fire under the microscope

How do you check if tools made of flint were used to kindle fire? When some objects of this kind were found in the Polish towns of Gródek and Ćmielów, some researchers from the city of Poznań first made exact copies of them and then spent ages patiently striking sparks over touchwood. They had to keep doing it over and over again, because the spark was often too small or entirely missed its target. Then they examined the original tools and their copies under a microscope to compare the changes that had occurred during rubbing and striking. Now they could tell which of the excavated tools were used to kindle fire and which to work stone.

French and Dutch scientists conducted a similar study of tools that came from various parts of France. As a result they demonstrated that not just Homo sapiens, but also Neanderthal man (Homo neanderthalensis) knew how to kindle fire 50,000 years ago.

SOURCE OF HEAT AND LIGHT

During combustion, energy is released in the form of light and heat. For hundreds of thousands of years people have made use of it in various ways, and because the need for it continued to grow, better techniques and kinds of fuel were constantly being designed, and new ones are still being developed today.

Wood

Wood is the easiest fuel to obtain. In many places it is used to heat houses. You are sure to be familiar with it from bonfires burned at campsites or in fireplaces.

Luchina, a piece of dried wood soaked in resin, was used for indoor lighting in Russia, Poland and Ukraine. In Poland traces of it have been found in places including Krzemionki Prehistoric Stiped Flint Mining region, which was already being mined in 3,900 BCE. And 150 years ago, luchina still lit up the interiors of rural cottages and underground passages.

COAL

LUCHINA

OIL LAMP

Fat

As the light of a bonfire could not reach into every corner of a large cave, people invented clever little lamps using animal fat. At first they simply drilled holes in stones to form little bowls, then placed dried moss soaked in fat in them and set it alight. In time they learned to make vessels out of clay, then bronze and other metals, which were used to make similar small lamps. They filled them with various kinds of oil, including olive oil. They also perfected their shape – to stop the fat from spilling, the lamps were closed at the top with just a small hole for the fuel to be poured inside, and another at the front for the wick. The candles familiar to you work on a similar basis, but in this case the wick is set in beeswax, paraffin or stearin, rather than olive oil.

Dung

Collecting cow pats is not a very pleasant task, but what can you do when you need warmth, but there's no wood or coal to hand? Fresh cow dung can be mixed with straw and formed into plate-size pats that are then dried in the sun. Once they've hardened they can be stacked in neat piles, like wood, by the fireplace. They burn easily and not very fast. This sort of fuel is used in some parts of Central Asia.

Coal

Coal, which is the ideal fuel, appears in nature in many different forms. It is formed over millions of years and mainly consists of an element called carbon. You can easily see carbon in the form of burned toast or charred twigs. When combined with hydrogen it forms **hydrocarbons**, such as crude oil, natural gas or diesel. When combined with hydrogen and oxygen it forms **carbohydrates**, which you know from the kitchen because they include sugar and starch.

Hard coal, oil, gas

To listen to music, talk on the phone or watch a movie we need electricity. Most of the world's electricity is still produced by power stations where fire is used to burn coal, oil or gas – in other words, **fossil fuels**. They were formed millions of years ago from the remains of animals or plants. Enormous ferns, trees and other plants slowly decomposed, forming peat, which as time passed was covered by successive layers of sand, clay and stone. Crushed under great pressure, the remains eventually changed into the hard, black, shiny rock that we call bituminous coal. Oil and gas were formed in a similar way from the remains of animals. All these raw materials are located deep underground and are heavily exploited. One day we might run out of them and then entire cities could be left without electricity. Besides, burning fossil fuels pollutes the environment. That's why people are constantly looking for new, more ecological sources of energy, and are making use of wind, water and sunlight.

CRUDE OIL   GAS

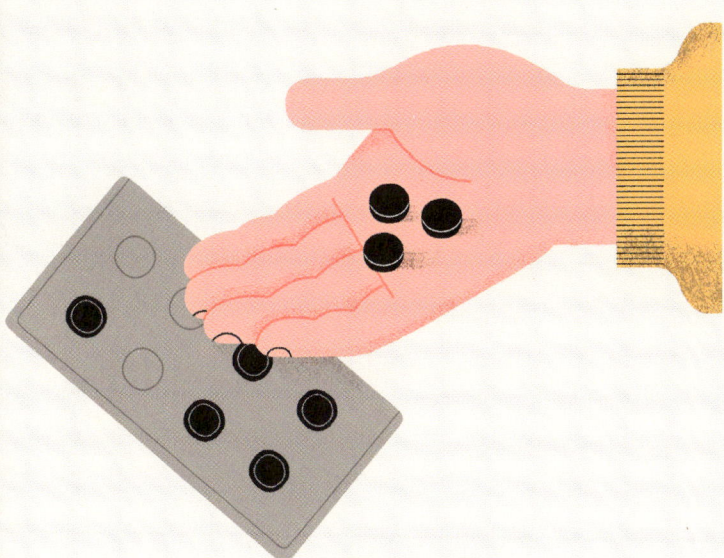

Ignacy Łukasiewicz (pronounced "Ignatsy Woo-kash-evich") was a Polish pharmacist who constructed an oil lamp that became a revolutionary invention. It didn't produce soot, it gave off strong light and was much cheaper than a gas lamp. Łukasiewicz worked at a pharmacy in Lwów (now Lviv in Ukraine), where in a small laboratory at the back he conducted experiments to clean oil. By applying a high temperature he managed to obtain pure oil, which could be used as fuel for the lamp he had designed.

Charcoal

Charcoal is made of wood that is burned in special ovens. It was used in ancient times, since then only the method for producing it has changed. It takes five kilogrammes of wood to produce just one kilogramme of charcoal. It doesn't give off as much smoke and it burns much more slowly, without high flames. That's why it is ideal for roasting meat and to this day is used for barbecues. And if you eat too much at a barbecue and suffer from a stomachache there are some special black pills that provide a good remedy, and they are also made of charcoal!

Lightbulb

In a lightbulb the wick has been replaced by a very durable, thin filament made of tungsten which does not burn, but emits an intense, bright light. It is supplied with energy by an electrical current.

BURNED ON A PYRE

Unfortunately, humankind has not always used fire in a positive way. There have been occasions in the past when it was deliberately used to kill and destroy.

Emil and the Detectives

If you like detective stories, read the story of a boy named Emil, who gets off a train at the station in Berlin but instead of going to his grandmother's house sets off in pursuit of a mysterious thief. When Erich Kästner wrote it in 1929, he had no idea that children all over the world would follow the boy's fortunes with bated breath. Nor could he have imagined the book would be burned on a pyre with thousands of other books that were banned in Nazi Germany. In the heart of Berlin, where Kästner's fictional hero Emil had his adventures, German students heaped up a huge pile of books in the square outside the Opera. The paper quickly caught fire and soon a large bonfire was burning, while the crowd continued to throw more books on to it. Many of them were excellent novels or wise works of philosophy by popular authors. Their only fault was that Hitler, the Nazi leader, refused to accept them. Now there is a monument in that spot on Bebelplatz. It's easy to overlook because it doesn't rise above the ground. To see it you have to bend over and look down. Underneath a thick square plate of glass set among the cobblestones you'll see an empty underground library. There's nothing on its shelves but the empty space where the burned books are missing.

"Although it does move"

So said the Italian astronomer Galileo Galilei, according to legend, when a church court forced him to revoke publicly his belief that the Earth revolves around the Sun. The church saw this idea as heresy. Galileo carried out the court's order, but apparently he added in a whisper: "Although it does move". He was not burned at the stake, he was only sentenced to house arrest, and his work was placed on the register of banned books.

Another Italian scientist Giordano Bruno was less fortunate. In 1592, he was imprisoned and after seven years in jail he was condemned to death for his views. He was tied to a stake and burned in a square in Rome called the Campo dei Fiori. Today, there is a monument to him there. You can't smell any smoke, just the pleasant aroma of spices, cheeses and homemade pesto for sale at the nearby market stalls. It was only in 2000 that Pope John Paul II apologised for the sins of the church court known as the Inquisition.

Warsaw, Poland

In the Summer of 1944, after the Warsaw Uprising (an operation by the Polish resistance to free Poland from German occupation), a special German army unit called the *Brandkommando* systematically set fire to every part of the city that had not been blown up during the military action. Soldiers armed with flamethrowers burned homes, historical buildings, schools and universities. They did not spare the valuable collections at the National Library. The library's books, maps and manuscripts were reduced to ashes. Some of them were 500 years old. Now the ashes of these priceless items are kept in a glass urn.

THE FIRE AGE

We've already had the Ice Age and the Iron Age, now get ready for the Fire Age, because the winter isn't coming. So warns American professor Stephen J. Pyne. Like many scientists, he thinks global warming can have an effect on the size and violence of fires.

Animals

The koala was moving awkwardly, it was clearly in pain and it had burned paws. It didn't even react to the noise of a braking vehicle, or to the firefighter who jumped out of it. It didn't try to run away, but sat helplessly, like a child, and let itself be given water from a bottle. It drank the water thirstily. Later it was taken to a shelter near Melbourne, where the vets bandaged its wounds, fed it, and put it in a pen that for some time would be its home. Many other animals were not so lucky. In the summer of 2009, thousands of koala bears were killed in forest fires. Usually they spend their time high up in eucalyptus trees. When danger comes, they usually save themselves by climbing higher and higher, but fire can climb, too, and eucalyptus trees quickly go up in flames. Slow-moving creatures like koalas have little chance of surviving.

Force

In Australia, droughts, heatwaves and wildfires are natural occurrences. They come and go. The farmers have their own security system in place. They make sure there is a buffer zone around their vast estates – a strip of land with no bushes, grass or trees that could burn. But lately the droughts and high temperatures have been so severe that fires can change into a force that's hard to control.

In February 2009 the thermometers showed 46.4°C. An absolute record! The earth was cracking for lack of water. A dry wind blew at a speed of 90 kmph, but instead of being refreshing it brought very hot air. In this hot weather a spark from a damaged power line was able to trigger a fire in a matter of seconds. The fire instantly turned entire stretches of forest into one big flaming torch, pouring out torrid heat over many kilometres. The local fire brigades were completely helpless. To make matters worse, firestorms appeared – intense fires, or conflagrations, that create their own wind system. In the Kilmore East region near Melbourne alone more than 125,000 hectares burned – that's almost double the size of the Kielder Forest in Northumberland!

Saturday 7th February 2009 went down in history as Black Saturday. Platypuses, cockatoos and even excellent runners such as kangaroos had no chance of escaping the fire, which killed more than a million animals both wild and domestic. And the ones that were saved lost their nests, dens, burrows and feeding grounds, places that couldn't be rebuilt quickly.

The firefighters noticed that previously heat ran a few hundred metres ahead of a fire, now it preceded it by as much as 10 kilometres, with flaming sparks jumping out of it, like bombs from a launcher. The fire spread faster and appeared in several places at once. People spotted a pillar of smoke far away on the horizon and just a few minutes later their houses were engulfed by fire! Just imagine one third of Poland on fire or an area larger than the whole of Great Britain – 100,000 square kilometres! That's how much terrain was destroyed by fire in Australia in 2019–2020.

During a firestorm there are powerful electric currents that act like a chimney, gushing smoke, dust and other pollutants into the stratosphere.

The pyrocumulonimbus cloud

Heated air rises from a bonfire, carrying sparks and bits of burning leaves. But what happens if the "bonfire" is several hectares in size? Then the temperature becomes unimaginably high and the air literally races upwards, sucking in sparks, smoke and dust. Huge, towering clouds form that move around, hurling bolts of lightning and igniting even more fire. The fire creates a storm, which destroys more terrain. It's accompanied by a very strong wind, but if you think that means pouring rain as well, you're wrong. Firestorms don't bring much rain, but the electric charges that come with them are very powerful. So there is fire shooting down from the sky as well as up from the earth.

Scientists argue that global warming is accompanied by more violent storms, greater droughts and more dramatic fires. Australia is not the only place where they are seeing evidence of this phenomenon. During August and September 2020, the sky over the San Francisco Bay Area in California took on an orange glow, as if the rays of the setting sun were illuminating it. But it wasn't the evening, no one was making their supper and the clocks were showing noon. Thick smoke blocked visibility and made it hard to breathe. It was fires that were colouring the sky. The dried-out vegetation was highly flammable and had caught fire at many sites simultaneously. People used a new word to describe it, calling it a "gigafire", because it raged over an incredibly large area for almost two months. Everything was at a record height: the temperature, the range, the drought, the quantity of smoke that obscured the sun and made day into night, and finally the number of fires. Altogether there were almost 1,000 of them.

Permafrost on fire

Fires can even occur in places where the ground is ice-bound for most of the year. In 2020 in Siberia, Russia, July was very unusual. There was no rain, the temperature was above 30°C and even beyond the Arctic Circle it was as high as 38°C. Fires broke out in several places at once. The fire latched on to dry sticks and leaf litter and was fuelled by the wind, which provided oxygen, and then the hot air drew the flames upwards. Very old trees soon turned into pillars of fire, and in no time an area larger than the country of Greece was alight.

These forests are home to deer, elk, badgers and even bears. Tits and waxwings bustle around in the trees and as evening falls owls set out hunting. Many of them did not survive that summer and the ones that did manage to escape the conflagration had nowhere to return to. The forest was completely destroyed. The most common trees in the taiga, as forests of this kind are called, are pines and spruces. Their trunks and branches are full of resin that protects them from freezing, but not from fire. Resinous wood burns easily, emitting sparks. The slender spruce trees grow for more than 20 years, but they burned up in a matter of hours.

Peat

Peat is not strictly a fossil fuel but is classified as a "solid fuel." It is formed in marshy areas from long-dead vegetation. While forests can burn quickly, peat burns very slowly and can still be glowing for several months. After the fires in Siberia, large peat bogs went on burning for a record length of time, even during severe winter frosts, polluting the atmosphere with numerous harmful gases.

PEAT

Migrating soot

How is it possible for soot from Australia to have reached North America and smoke from fires in California to have flown all the way to New York? Hot air rises quickly, gathering dust and soot. At a great height it encounters air currents that flow like a rapid stream, carrying off harmful substances and transporting them across thousands of kilometres. Soot from fires in the Canadian taiga was carried by the wind all the way to Greenland, where it settled on glaciers, creating dark stains. They in turn absorb solar energy and contribute to climate change.

Dragon's eggs

When fires are as big as the ones in California or Australia fighting them is like a vast military operation. It starts in outer space. Warning systems make use of photos and data sent by satellites for monitoring regions at risk of fires. This information helps to provide rapid warning when a fire erupts.

Once it is burning, an enormous part of the operation takes place in the air. Drones are sent to the most dangerous, smoke-filled spots without risking the firefighter's lives. Their cameras film terrain that no human can possibly fly into, and the pictures are immediately sent to computer screens at command centres. As a result, the people coordinating the work of hundreds of firefighters, machines and volunteers know in which direction the fire is heading and how big it is. They can send the right help to the right place.

And so tankers fly out. Tankers are huge aeroplanes that can carry from 15,000 to more than 40,000 litres of water. They open their tanks above the area that's on fire and pour down the water. They can't descend too low, so helicopters join the operation, too. They can fly into places that the tankers can't reach. They, too, have a system for pouring and sprinkling water. They cannot carry as much water as an aeroplane (only 1,000-7,000 litres), but they

When the Australian bush burned, 3,400 firefighters, more than 3,000 soldiers and a huge crowd of volunteers battled the flames. In many places they simply worked to stop the fire from spreading to a wider area.

can target precisely, by hovering in one spot. They can also turn around easily and quickly replenish their water supplies. They can release hosepipes, which give them a simple way to collect water from lakes, for instance. Planes and helicopters are also used for dry fire extinguishing. They release foam or chemical fluids in places the fire hasn't yet reached, and that can stop it from spreading.

At the same time drones, are sent out without cameras, but equipped with "dragon's egg" launchers. These are small spheres that look like table-tennis balls. When they hit the ground they explode, creating small, controlled fires. Their job is to burn off potential concentrations of dry bushes and grass, so that the massive fire approaching will have nothing to feed on.

So most of the assistance comes from the air. Meanwhile on the ground, hundreds of firefighters fight the fire, evacuating the inhabitants and helping animals. They take their machines to places the fire has not yet reached, where they dig ditches that will stop its advance. Meteorologists keep track of changes in the wind direction and the weather forecast. They send all this data to the command centre, because the weather can help or hinder a firefighting operation.

Can fire combat fire?

Every year people come from all over the world to hike in the Yosemite National Park and to admire the world's tallest trees – the sequoias. These giants can reach 100 metres in height, almost as high as a 27-storey tower block! They grow in California, where there is a high risk of forest fires. Yet their wardens deliberately start fires there that cover an area as large as 70 football pitches! Weird? They have their reasons.

Sequoias are incredibly resistant to fire. Their trunks are covered in hard, armour-like bark that's half a metre thick. It doesn't let flames or heat get inside the tree to where its life-giving sap is flowing. As a result, the tree can survive. Meanwhile, it turns out that fire can not only destroy but can also help to create new life. Sequoia cones only open if they're exposed to a high temperature. Sometimes squirrels help by splitting the cones, which are harder than nuts, but the seeds are only fully scattered thanks to the heat emitted during a fire. A fire that is started deliberately does not slip out of control, but burns up a lot of dead branches, dry twigs and tree stumps that cannot be removed in any other way. If they were left on the forest floor, large piles of them would accumulate, which would be the perfect fuel for wildfires. And then even such mighty trees as the sequoias would be in danger.

What can a little beaver do to fight the flames? Not much, if a conflagration is already approaching, but the work of these clever creatures is often more effective than an expensive fire-prevention plan. Beavers build dams, make ponds and dig canals. Within their environment they create a special water system that protects plants and animals from fire. Sometimes it can even stop a fire from advancing.

HOW NOT TO GET BURNED

Anyone who has sat around the campfire until late at night will know how pleasant it is to gaze into the flames, sing songs, and toast bread or sausages. At such times we never think about major fires. But it's good to know the **safety rules**. A forest fire destroys trees, bushes, moss, grass and flowers. It kills animals, and the ones that survive lose their source of food and their home. Smoke, ash and lots of other pollutants poison the air. In the United States negligent people are still to blame for most forest fires, which start because of their carelessness.

A safe campfire

Do not light a bonfire close to trees or bushes. Be especially careful if there's a drought, because that's when it only takes a spark to cause a conflagration.

Clear away the leaves and dry grass around the bonfire site. You can also surround it with stones, so the flames won't spread.

Once your evening is coming to an end, carefully pour water over the bonfire. Don't leave any embers or the wind might carry off sparks during the night.

Don't leave rubbish in the forest. Don't drop bits of paper, which easily burns, and be careful not to leave glass behind because it can kindle fire by focusing the rays of the sun.

COLLECTED RUBBISH

CIRCLE OF STONES

WATER FOR EXTINGUISHING

How do you extinguish a fire?

To put out a fire, you must deprive it of oxygen or energy (a high temperature). **Water** is usually very effective. It lowers the temperature and when it comes into contact with fire it changes into steam, which displaces oxygen. The stream of water is aimed straight at the flames, and the surrounding area is also soaked, so the fire cannot spread.

BUT BEWARE, not every fire can be put out by water! Never pour water on burning oil, because it spatters or even explodes and spreads the fire, and it can burn you. If fat starts to burn in a frying pan, call an adult immediately! You should switch off the burner underneath it, tightly cover the pan with a lid and leave it in place until the pan cools down. It can also help to sprinkle a large amount of **salt** on the oil.

DO NOT pour water on any burning object plugged into an electrical outlet. Immediately ask an adult for help! In this situation, the plug must be removed from the outlet, *if it is safe to do so*. The supply of electricity can also be turned off at the fuse box. And there are special extinguishers that can be used for electrical fires.

Sand is ideal for cutting off the oxygen and preventing splashes, though it cannot be used to put out burning oils or petroleum, as sand melts in burning liquids.

Foams, powders and gases

What can fire extinguishers extinguish? It all depends on their chemical composition. To make it easier, they are colour coded, and fires are put into different categories that indicate the type of fire they can extinguish.

Class A – caused by flammable solids, such as wood, paper and fabric
Class B – caused by flammable liquids, like petrol or paint
Class C – caused by flammable gases, such as hydrogen or methane
Class D – caused by combustible metals and chemicals such as magnesium or potassium
Class E – caused by electrical items, like heaters, computers or phone chargers
Class F – caused by cooking oils

47

What can fire do to the human body?

Lungs

During a fire **smoke** is produced, which is a mixture of gases and tiny specks of burning materials. These particles are several dozen times smaller than a grain of sand and can easily get into the lungs. And then the body treats them like an enemy and activates its defence system, just as it would to fight a virus. Unfortunately our immunological cells can't destroy solids, so they simply try to work harder and harder to counteract them. Eventually an inflammatory condition arises and sometimes permanent damage to the lungs. Quite often burning objects emit toxic gases. If you have to force your way through clouds of smoke, it's best to cover your mouth and nose with a wet rag or a face mask. Remember that smoke rises, so if you bend over you have a chance of inhaling a lower concentration of toxins.

Skin

The skin forms a barrier between us and the world, protecting us from illnesses and infections. It is responsible for maintaining the right body temperature. Fire can harm or even destroy it. It all depends on the level of the burn, which is defined by degrees:

First-degree burns harm the outer layer, or epidermis, which turns extremely red.

Second-degree burns reach the inner layer of the skin. Blisters appear and the spot is very painful.

Third-degree burns damage the skin and destroy blood vessels, synapses (nerve connections) and receptors, which pass information to the brain, and that disturbs the functioning of the entire body. In this case medical help is essential.

Fourth-degree burns char the flesh.

If you ever get burned, you must quickly put the burned part of your body into cold water for several minutes. Don't smear grease or cream on the burn – use special foam for burns if you have it.

THIRD-DEGREE BURN

FOURTH-DEGREE BURN

A human torch
If someone's clothes catch fire, that person must instantly be rolled on the ground and covered with a blanket, jacket or thick piece of cloth to put out the fire, and then an ambulance must be called at once. DO NOT use artificial material to extinguish the flames, or it will melt and stick to the body.

A fire-resistant suit
Firefighters sometimes have to carry people or animals out of burning buildings, and that means they must literally jump into the fire. They are protected from high temperatures and flames by special suits. They also use oxygen cylinders, because at the heart of a fire there is no air to breathe.

Help
If you ever witness a fire, you must immediately call **999**. **Calmly and clearly** state what is on fire. Give the address, your full name and phone number. **Don't hang up** until you hear that your report has been received!

49

FIRE WORSHIP

Flames move violently, racing from place to place, devouring whatever stands in their way like a wild animal. Sometimes flames look as if they are alive. No wonder people have always been afraid of them, and also in awe of them. In ancient times, fire, which came from the sky in the form of lightning or from underground during a volcanic eruption, was associated with divine power. And in various parts of the world it was worshipped like a god, or like a gift from the gods.

In the temples of ancient Greece and Rome a fire burned in honour of the gods. For the Greeks the goddess Hestia was protector of the domestic hearth, and her sacred fire was kept burning in Delphi. The Romans called her Vesta. The guardians of the fire, known as the vestal virgins, had to be very careful not to let the fire go out, because that particular mistake would cost them their lives.

In pre-Christian Ireland, at a place called Kildare the inhabitants kept a fire burning in honour of the Celtic goddess Brigid, and asked her to give them good harvests and to protect their livestock. Later on, the Christian Saint Brigid founded a convent there, where the nuns kept a sacred fire burning as a symbol of the presence of Christ.

On the evening of Easter Saturday when Christians are waiting for Easter Sunday, the day when Jesus rose from the dead, the priest lights a bonfire outside the church entrance. They light a candle from the consecrated fire and carry it into the dark church. There they give the light to the congregation, and they pass it on to one another until the whole church is filled with shimmering brightness.

In the Old Testament, God reveals Himself to Moses in the form of a burning bush that is never consumed by the fire.

The Festival of Lights

The Jewish holiday, Hanukkah, also known as Hag-ha-Urim, which means "the festival of lights", lasts for eight days. On each day, one candle is lit and allowed to burn for at least half an hour. On the last day, by which time there are nine candles burning in a special candelabra called a menorah (the candle in the middle is used to light all the others), the Jews prepare a festive supper at which families gather and exchange gifts. They serve specially made deep-fried potato pancakes and doughnuts. The tradition dates back to the rising of the Maccabees against the Syrian king. After the victory, religious Jews wanted to light an oil lamp in the temple in Jerusalem. They could only find one, and to make matters worse, there was hardly any oil left in it. They thought it would soon go out, but it went on burning for eight days. Hanukkah regularly coincides with the Christmas holiday, and thus with the winter solstice, the shortest day of the year.

SAINT LUCY'S DAY

Every year a festival of light is held in Sweden on 13 December to commemorate Saint Lucy's day. Lucy lived in Sicily in the fourth century. But the joyful celebrations do not have much to do with her. After dark, people go out into the streets in processions headed by girls or women dressed in white. Everyone carries a lighted lantern or candle, and the young woman at the head of the procession wears a crown of flaming candles on her head.

At the time of the longest day in the year, when summer is approaching, Midsummer Eve is celebrated. People might watch the sunrise, tell stories and dance all night. In the past there were bonfires, too, and the young men jumped over them to show off their agility and courage. The girls floated garlands of flowers with burning candles on the rivers, believing that if the garland floated a long way but the flame stayed alight, the girl would soon be married.

Diwali, the Hindu festival of lights, lasts for five days, during which the victory of good over evil is celebrated. Houses and shop windows are illuminated by all sorts of lanterns and oil lamps, and fireworks light up the sky.

THE OLYMPIC FLAME

No one is ever allowed to take fire on board an aeroplane, unless it's the Olympic flame. It can travel! It flies safely, secured by belts, on an assigned seat like any other passenger. It is locked inside a special lantern that has a guardian – a firefighter who sits next to it. But it rarely travels by plane. It sets off from Olympia in Greece, where it is lit from the sun's rays before each Olympic Games. Then some of the competing athletes perform a relay, carrying a torch lit by the flame on foot or by transport until it reaches the place where the games are being held. During the opening ceremony one of the athletes runs into the stadium carrying the torch and lights the Olympic cauldron, which will burn until the end of the competition.

In ancient Greece the Olympic Games were held at Olympia, so there was no need to transport the flame. The idea of the torch relay only began in 1936, when the games were held in Munich, Germany.

56

Before the 2014 Winter Olympic Games in Sochi, Russia, the flame briefly ended up 13 metres underwater in Lake Baikal. How was it kept burning? It had a special burner designed for it, which allowed it to stay alight underwater. On another occasion the Olympic flame visited the ocean depths near the Great Barrier Reef. That time it was heading to Sydney, Australia in 2000.

The Olympic flame has been to the North Pole, the northernmost point in the world, and the torch – though without fire – has also been in outer space, where it was taken by Russian cosmonauts! Its ways of reaching its destination vary, but the main point of the torch relay is to spread a message of peace.

The ancient Olympic Games were a sporting and religious ceremony in one. The athletes competed in honour of the god Zeus. Women were not allowed to take part in the competition, or even to enter the stadium but they could take part in the Heraean Games, dedicated to the goddess Hera. The first sporting games took place in Olympia in 776 BCE, and the last of the ancient games took place in 394 CE. They were only revived in the nineteenth century, in 1896, in Athens, Greece. The winter games were held for the first time in 1924.

FIERY CREATURES

Who breathes fire in the fairy tales? Dragons, of course. In many countries there are legends featuring these large and dangerous creatures. A dragon named Smaug was greedy; he liked gold and precious gemstones. He knew that the most fabulous jewels were to be found in the kingdom of the dwarves, so he attacked their settlements, flooding them with fire and utterly destroying them. The only thing he saved was their treasure, and from then on he guarded it. Many years later 12 dwarves, one hobbit and one wizard set off on a dangerous journey to recover the lost kingdom. Their adventures were described by J. R. R. Tolkien in *The Hobbit: or There and Back Again*.

The Chronicles of Narnia feature an unusual dragon who really did enjoy breathing fire, but not in order to kill. He had no trouble lighting people's bonfires for them, even when made of the wettest wood, and on chilly evenings he provided warmth with his hot breath.

The Wawel dragon is familiar to every child in Poland. They go to visit it underneath the royal castle in Kraków. Apparently, long, long ago it lived there in a cave and devoured people. Today it behaves well, only breathing fire on request. It is a bronze sculpture designed and made by Bronisław Chromy (pronounced "Bron-ees-wuff Hroamy").

SMAUG

THE DRAGON FROM NARNIA

THE WAWEL DRAGON

Dragon warrior
In the movie *Kung Fu Panda* the hero is not a dragon, but a dragon warrior. His task is to bring security and harmony to the valley. This American movie shows a Chinese tradition in which dragons are good creatures that prompt admiration rather than fear. They are a symbol of power and good fortune and are not in the habit of setting anything alight with their breath. On the contrary, they rule the rivers, seas and rain.

There are real dragons living in Indonesia. They are the biggest lizards on earth, can grow up to 3 metres long, and can kill their enemy with a blow of their tail. These are the Komodo dragons. Tourists can see them at the Komodo National Park. But they have to be careful, because although the dragons don't breathe fire, they can be dangerous and might attack.

In legend, salamanders were born in fire and lived in the hot embers. Real salamanders live in forests and like to hide in rocky recesses or between the roots of trees. They have damp, shiny black skin with yellow or orange patches. Apparently in the past they were often seen slithering from under branches tossed into the fire. This was the source of the fantastical stories about lizard-like creatures that love fire.

The phoenix, on the other hand, only exists in legends. The ancient Egyptians believed that these unusual birds had golden-red plumage. They sang tunefully and could live for as long at 500 years, but always in solitude, because throughout the world there was only one phoenix at a time. When its life was coming to an end, the phoenix built itself a funeral pyre out of sticks and twigs that it set on fire before dying in its flames. Then a new bird was born out of the ashes. You probably remember Fawkes, the magical bird who belonged to the wizard Albus Dumbledore in the Harry Potter books.

FAMOUS FIRES
London

In seventeenth century London the wooden houses stood so close together that you only had to lean out of the window to shake your neighbour's hand. The roofs were covered with flammable straw. In 1666, the summer was extremely hot, and it hadn't rained for days on end. Some of the wells were empty, and the streets, usually wet, were coated in dust.

One September night a fire broke out at Thomas Farriner's bakery. The dry floor and walls of the building instantly began to burn. Soon flames were belching through the straw roof straight into the dark sky, and the wind sent sparks and burning splinters flying. Waking in terror, the residents summoned help. The church bells sounded the alarm, but in those days London had no fire brigade. So the neighbours helped. But what could they do with nothing but water in leather buckets? They tried pulling the straw off the roofs to stop the fire but it wasn't much use. The dry wood and straw were consumed in an instant. Roof after roof, wall after wall, house after house changed into a pillar of fire. Smoke covered the sky. To make matters worse, a strong, dry wind blew the sparks far and wide. In panic the citizens harnessed their carts and tried to save their possessions. Samuel Pepys, who described the whole event, buried his wine and parmesan cheese, very valuable products that were hard to obtain.

The fire destroyed large parts of the city, and many families lost everything they owned. Soon after, the first insurance companies were formed in London, which trained their own firefighting services, a bit like the first fire brigades. Except that when summoned to help they only put out the fire at the buildings that had a sign stating that they had bought a policy from the relevant insurance company. It was even worse in ancient Rome. When the firefighters arrived on the spot, they waited for a suitable financial offer from the owner of the building. If they weren't satisfied, they just stood there watching while the house burned down.

Rome

Did you know that a fire can melt nails and they can survive underground for hundreds of years? During an excavation in Rome, Clementina Panelle, an Italian archaeologist, discovered a charred gateway, pieces of a collapsed stone wall and melted nails. She and her team excavated the site where almost 2,000 years ago the Great Fire of Rome broke out, before spreading and destroying the whole city. In those days this area was inhabited by the poor and was a long way from the stone buildings of the Forum at the city centre. So how could the fire have reached the stone-built part of the city and destroyed it?

Tacitus, a historian who was alive at the time of the fire, believed that the emperor Nero was responsible for the fire because he wanted to destroy the rich city centre. Previously, he had wanted to rebuild it, but the Senate (the legislative assembly) had refused to give its consent, so he had the city set on fire. But modern historians and archaeologists researching that era do not necessarily agree with Tacitus. The melted nails could be evidence to Nero's advantage. As you know, the greater a fire, the faster the air rises and is replaced by cooler air that provides oxygen. The oxygen reinforces the fire and increases air movement, in other words the wind. The fact that the nails melted proves that the temperature must have been very high and the fire really did go wild. So the heated air could have carried sparks all the way to the Forum.

Notre-Dame

The most famous cathedral in France was constructed over a period of almost 200 years, from the twelfth to the fourteenth century. First the old church and surrounding buildings were demolished. The area changed into a huge building site with many workshops. In those days there were no cranes, diggers or drills. Yet all the latest technical and architectural solutions were applied there. The cathedral was to eclipse every other building as the most modern and graceful of all. It seemed eternal.

In 2019, renovation work was being carried out inside the cathedral. Workmen were walking around wooden scaffolding. The vault, the skeleton of which consisted of mighty oak beams, was undergoing conservation. On 15 April at around 6:30 p.m. a fire broke out. The dry timber was quickly engulfed. The surrounding area was hard to enter because the cathedral is surrounded by narrow streets and the main way into the square was blocked by concrete anti-terrorist barriers. While the fire engines were struggling to reach the spot, the ancient beams rapidly burned. The whole world was watching when at 7:53 p.m. the 40-metre spire collapsed, followed 14 minutes later by the roof. Luckily at around midnight the fire was brought under control.

FIRE IN OUTER SPACE

If you wanted to go from London to Sydney, you'd have to travel nearly 17,000 kilometres, and on a journey from the Earth to the Moon you'd go almost 400,000. But no one has ever tried travelling to the Sun because they'd have to overcome two basic obstacles: a distance of 150 million kilometres and a temperature of 5,700°C. It is colloquially called a "fireball", but it's not a combination of oxygen and carbon that is burning there. There are no flames. The Sun consists of very hot gases and it is a star, like many others in the cosmos. But for us it is unique because it constantly provides us with energy in the form of light. Its radiation prompts atoms to move faster and vibrate more; in other words, it makes the environment hot. It is thanks to the Sun that life exists on Earth.

The temperature on the surface of the Sun is as high as 5,700°C, but inside it goes up to 16 million°C. The Sun is so big that a million planets the size of Earth could fit inside it. Its light reaches us in about 8 minutes. It came into being 4.6 billion years ago.

SUN   EARTH

Solar panels transform the energy from the Sun into electricity. They can be tiny, like the ones in calculators or watches, or immense, like the ones that power batteries for the International Space Station, for example.

RA

HELIOS

APOLLO

TONATIUH

Ra was the god of the Sun. The ancient Egyptians regarded him as the creator and giver of life. They believed that every morning he sailed on a special boat from east to west and then, at the end of the day, he went underground. In ancient Greece, Helios drove a chariot, but in Greek mythology you are more likely to read about a different sun god, Apollo. Meanwhile the Aztecs worshipped Tonatiuh, "He who shines and gives warmth". He was the god of the Sun and of warriors. They believed he must be fed with human blood or else his light would go out.

CURIOUS FACTS

A flash of lightning that stretched over a distance of 709 kilometres was recorded in South America. It ran from Argentina right across Brazil, all the way to the Atlantic coast. Another record-breaker lasted for 16.74 seconds. Start a timer and imagine one single flash of lightning illuminating the sky outside your window for all that time.

Are there really birds that set fire to the meadows in the Australian savannah? It sounds like something out of a fantasy novel, but it's true. For centuries the indigenous inhabitants of Australia observed the behaviour of kites and hawks that picked up burning twigs in their beaks or talons and then dropped them on dry meadows, causing a fire. Until recently these stories were regarded as myth, but now it is known that the birds really do start fires to flush out the small reptiles and rodents they are hunting.

A record temperature of 56.6°C was recorded on 10 July 1913 in Death Valley, an extremely hot, dry part of the Mojave Desert.

The Empire State Building, New York's most famous skyscraper, is struck by lightning 100 times each year.

During large forest fires the temperature can be as high as 1,000°C, or higher.

The American scientist and politician Benjamin Franklin attracted lightning with the help of a kite, a piece of string and a key. In the process he proved that it is a form of electricity. Further experiments helped him to invent the lightning conductor.

On 11 September 2001, when two passenger planes hit the twin towers of the World Trade Center in New York, 343 firefighters were killed in the rescue operation. It wasn't an accident, but a carefully planned terrorist attack. Thousands of people had to be evacuated from the burning towers.

The firebird is featured in Russian fables. Its tail was aflame with real fire, but it didn't burn up and it had great magical power. The Russian composer Igor Stravinsky wrote the music for the ballet *The Firebird*, which can be heard at concert halls worldwide.

An eternal flame burns in many places worldwide to commemorate important historical or religious events. It is usually in the form of a large torch that never goes out. In Europe, there is one in The Hague, at the Peace palace, dedicated to the idea of international peace.

BOXER BOOKS and the distinctive Boxer Books logo are trademarks of Hachette Book Group, Inc., Carmelite House, 50 Victoria Embankment, London, UK, EC4Y 0DZ.
EU address: Hachette Ireland, 8 Castlecourt Centre, Castleknock Road, Castleknock, Dublin 15, D15 XTP3, Republic of Ireland; e-mail: info@hbgi.ie

Originally published as *Ogień* by Muchomor, Warsaw, 2022
Polish text © 2022 Anna Skowrońska
Illustrations © 2022 Agata Dudek and Małgorzata Nowak (Acapulco Studio)
English translation © 2026 Antonia Lloyd-Jones
English translation rights arranged through KaBooks rights agency – Karolina Jaszecka

All rights reserved. No part of this publication may be reproduced, stored in a retrieval system, or transmitted in any form or by any means (including electronic, mechanical, photocopying, recording, or otherwise) without prior written permission from the publisher.

This edition first published in Great Britain in 2026 by Boxer Books.

ISBN 978-1-4547-1272-5

A catalogue record of this book is available from the British Library.

Boxer Books titles may be purchased in bulk for business, educational, or promotional use.
For more information, please contact your local bookseller or the Hachette Book Group's Special Markets department at special.markets@hbgusa.com.

Printed in China

10 9 8 7 6 5 4 3 2 1

11/25

unionsquareandco.com